Library of Congress Cataloging-in-Publication Data is available upon request.
Library of Congress Control Number: 2021918879

ISBN: 978-1-952357-38-1

Contact:
hello@alabasterco.com
www.alabasterco.com

Alabaster Co explores the intersection of creativity, beauty, and faith. Founded in 2016.
Based in Los Angeles.

TOWARDS
REST

CONTENTS

——

INTRODUCTION

We live in an age of busyness. Markets tune our lives to the pace of consumption and production. Daily, we are pulled by the persuasions of productivity, performance, and prestige. The common forces of exploitation and convenience dictate our social and economic arrangements. For new, old, and evermore reasons, we are chronically averse to rest.

God rests. From the very beginning, rest is marked with sacred significance among all of creation and the creative process. God calls individuals and communities alike into lives, rhythms, and conventions of rest. More than a mere afternoon nap, rest is a holy orientation and divine chronology that completes life as we know it. Just as God rests, we rest with God.

On this matter, God's way of life is stridently opposed to that of the world's. In rest, we witness a clash between stillness and hurry, calm and anxiety, and freedom and exploitation. However gentle in its appearance, rest is no small thing. Rest calls forth worship, play, and liberation. Rest reacquaints us with our souls, our environment, and our relationships. Rest enables us to thrive amid crisis, fortifying our resistance against the constant and cruel patterns of oppression and overproduction that dominate our world.

Why does God rest, and why are we called to rest as well? How does rest influence our character, relationships, and contributions to the world? What is a more restful world like? This book is meant to move us *towards rest*, into recovering its wisdom and consequence in our lives. In it, we consider rest and its relationship to God, awareness, resilience, play, community, pace, and changing the world.

As we contemplate and practice these many qualities of rest, may our personal lives be rejuvenated, our families strengthened, and our communities reoriented towards justice and peace. And may we rest with God. Amen.

01
Rest & God

Introduction

"We can't say yes to everything. We can't go everywhere and see everyone. We can't have it all. We aren't indispensable. We are beings who need rest. And that is not a bad thing. It is a Godlike thing."
– Adele Ahlberg Calhoun[1]

Rest is a *Godlike thing*. When we rest, we are doing something sacred. Rest is at the heart of being *with God*.

In the beginning, God created the universe: the stars, the oceans, the mountains, and us. This creative endeavor included resting and proclaiming that what God had formed was *good*. When we, as God's people, rest, we continue his creative precedent from eons ago. In rest, we are drawn back to the beginning, to the Creator.

Resting with God holds power and significance beyond relaxing or refueling ourselves. It is a way of declaring to ourselves, to the world, and to our Maker, that it is *good* for us to be offline, playful, and unproductive. It releases us from remaining bonded to the day's labor, enabling us to remember our dependence on God. Indeed, rest unlocks our unhealthy obsession with ourselves, our worries, and our idols, and allows us to partake in true humanity: playing with our children, remaining present to others, or simply breathing and delighting in nature.

We tend to resist rest because it counters social and market values of hurry, productivity, and purpose. We insist on resting when the work is *done*—but find there is always more to do. What if we changed our view of rest, so that it was not merely a stepping stone to the next goal post? What if it was not seen as lazy or self-indulgent, but profoundly meaningful and formative for ourselves, our relationships, and our communities?

Rest can transport us to an inner peace amid the most tumultuous storms. Rest can provide an honest assessment of our many burdens. Rest transfers our gaze from schedules to soul, where problems do not disappear but pale beside the aching appetite to be *with God*.

God Rests

All rest begins with the reality that *God* rests. God is the Author, Creator, and Center of rest—and models rest for us.

In Genesis 2, God finishes creating and rests. First introduced as creative and powerful, God is quickly depicted as valuing and practicing rest. "Then God blessed the seventh day and made it holy, because on it he rested from all the work of creating that he had done" (Gen. 2:3 NIV). Rest is a hallowed experience of remembrance. God models not

only how to rest, but how to *understand* rest. Rest is not merely a matter of routine, but a proclamation of goodness. God models rest as a *choice*. God does not solely rest from tiredness or necessity, but because it is simply worth it.

We do not often "bless" our times of rest, nor understand them as containing existential wisdom. Instead, our idols of work, money, and self frame rest as mere fuel towards future work. We understand rest as machines might, bereft of intimate connection to our Creator. This framing keeps rest to minimal, unspiritual importance in our life. We only rest when we feel we absolutely need to—when we are worn out and tired. This cycle leaves us beholden and bound to the same idols, instead of thriving in divine connection to God.

God encounters us in rest, and rest helps us concede our *cen-ter* to God. In rest, we acknowledge that we are not of central importance in our lives, families, and world—but God is. In rest, we upset the common falsehood that production is the central engine of our lives. In rest, our days, weeks, and years contain a new cadence. As detailed in the creation story, God is the central energy, meaning, and love binding all of creation together. Rest helps us remember this. We remember we are animated dust, woven into beautiful relationship with all of creation by a Creator that rests. We are meant for much more than we often believe.

Designed for Dependence

The central problem of our fractured world, some say, is the lie of *independence*. We view ourselves as sorts of *gods*—fundamentally independent, self-reliant creatures free of truly *needing* God. We raise ourselves and our work to utmost importance. Our culture implicitly reinforces this, reminding us that our importance is located mostly in what we *do*. In rest, we locate ourselves in the truth that we are meant for more than production, and that all our work must be done in partnership with God.

Living away from Eden, we are inundated with messages that we are entirely responsible for our success, our failures, our wellbeing, our relationships, and more. When we grow up, we are expected to care for ourselves and others. We aren't encouraged to ask for help. Independence numbs and diminishes our humanity—that we are fundamentally designed to be dependent on God.

Rest reminds us of this. Not merely a mundane practice, rest helps us remember our identities as heavenly children—not employees—in human bodies. Pastor Adele Calhoun writes, "We are citizens of another kingdom—a kingdom not ruled by the clock and the tyranny of the urgent."[2] Moving from self-importance to dependence on God can release joy in us. We are not meant to be self-sufficient or carry the world on our shoulders; we are meant for dependence, rest, and play. In rest, we acknowledge that God works when we do not. The psalmist writes, "Your eyes saw my unformed body; all the days ordained for me were written in your book before one of them came to be" (Ps. 139:16 NIV). If we look closely, we too can see the spirals of his fingerprints on the hours of our days.

Learning to rest is *relearning dependence.* This is a spiritual discipline, requiring time. Resting begins in divine allowance, acknowledging that rest is okay, natural, good—that we are designed for it. As dependent beings, we can trust in God and loosen our grip on life.

Rest does not inhibit life from happening. A family member might fall sick, an opportunity may expire, or a disaster could ensue. Resting means acknowledging things will be missed, lost, and broken in our absence, but that we will emerge afterwards still whole, loveable, and loved. Rest involves trusting that things will hold without our constant care and maintenance, that relationships will continue even when time has passed, that everything will all be all right.

In the book *How To Do Nothing*, author Jenny Odell writes: "When overstimulation has become a fact in life, I suggest that we reimagine #FOMO as #NOMO—the necessity of missing out, or if that bothers you, #NOSMO, the necessity of sometimes missing out."[3] Being available, or showing up all the time, does not prevent bad things from happening—it only exhausts us until we are fatigued and prone to resentment and temptation.

In Matthew 8, Jesus and his disciples find themselves in the middle of a storm with waves big enough that they swept over the boat. When they look at Jesus, he is sleeping. The disciples, afraid of death, wake Jesus up; he immediately calms the storm and chastises the men saying, "You of little faith, why are you so afraid?" (Matt. 8:26 NIV). Jesus' trust in God allowed him to relax to the point where he could do something as impossible as sleep during a storm. As we begin our journeys back to rest, may God give us the courage to lean back in his always open and available arms.

"I lay down and slept, yet I woke up in safety, for the LORD was watching over me." – Ps. 3:5 NLT

The Sabbath

At the core of a rich spiritual life with God is *The Sabbath*. Born of God's seventh day's rest, Sabbath instructs us not to work—not as a punishment, but as a gift. On Sabbaths, we recall that God is our center, we are designed to rest, and that goodness happens even when we do not labor for it. We recognize that miracles and gifts are bestowed upon us, not because we earned them or even wished for them, but because we are our God's beloved creation.

The practice of Sabbath may differ from one person to another, just as our relationships to God involve diverse expressions and practices. Sabbath may involve praying, sleeping, exercising, delighting, or simply being. In her book *Spiritual Disciplines*, Calhoun suggests Sabbaths include "letting go of things that stress you out for 24 hours, letting the difficult conversations happen another day, and not developing a to-do list."[4] Sabbath, and rest more broadly, is not about ignoring important and challenging things; it is about being

recentered on God, breathing, and allowing life to wait. On Sabbath, we are present— but not unaware of the impending future, but choosing to remain tuned to the present moment of resting with God.

Sabbath teaches us patience. It humbles us. It guides us gently back to dust, where we are smaller than the sequoias God erected decades before us, where we are younger than the mountains we climb on weekends, where we are adults in progress and in need of love, support, and relationship. Sabbath recenters us on the mystery of our faith, our roots, our heritage. It reminds us of creation and Creator.

On Sabbath, time is different. When we return to ourselves in slowness, we realize the world around us is vibrant, lively, and delightful. We recognize all we've missed: the sounds of birds and wind, the tightness of our muscles, the enduring sensations of our soul. On Sabbath, we walk back to ourselves on a trail paved since the dawn of creation—taking one more step on a journey towards rest.

"In peace I will lie down and sleep, for you alone, LORD, make me dwell in safety." – Ps. 4:8 NIV

02
Rest & Awareness

Introduction

We are designed with capacity for sensation and perception. A murmuring stomach signals hunger to us. Aching muscles remind us to stretch after exercise. Desire for connection motivates us to make plans with our friends. But however innate these pathways of awareness, the demands of this world render us ignorant of our physical, emotional, and spiritual needs.

We neglect our cues to rest. We strain our bodies beyond their limits. We avoid our anxieties by mindlessly plunging ourselves into content. We consume caffeine and supplements to avoid collapse. Rather than drinking from the "living water" (John 4:1-15) of God, we nourish ourselves with the things of this world without realizing that they worsen our ability to truly rest.

Being unaware of our need to rest can beget disobedience to God, consequence, and even death. When we remain willfully unaware of the gracious blessings of God, we grumble over our labor and daily stressors. We easily fixate on what we do not have, and forget all that we *do* have. In Psalm 127:2 NRSV, David proclaims, "It is in vain that you rise up early and go late to rest, eating the bread of anxious toil; for he gives sleep to his beloved." This vain rat race after the wind strips us from the joy of the present—even the basic gift of sleep.

When we are not aware of God, we wither and experience lostness. When we are not aware of sin, we fall prone to temptation. When we are not aware of the present, we deceive ourselves with desperate plans to fill our longing hearts—the very place where God is often missing.

When we are too impatient to wait, we miss the better doors that God opens for us. We believe the common falsehood that we must work harder to achieve meaning, or else we are left disappointed and incapable. Ultimately, we fear that by resting from all manner of labor, we will cease to prove our worthiness of being loved by actions, accomplishments, and acclaim.

This cruel lie provokes our restlessness, leading us to forget who we are. It leaves many without awareness that they are enough, deeply loved by a God whose arms remain open to them.

"Come to me, all who labor and are heavy laden, and I will give you rest. Take my yoke upon you, and learn from me, for I am gentle and lowly in heart, and you will find rest for your souls. For my yoke is easy, and my burden is light." – Matt. 11:28-30 ESV

Awareness of Breath

The most vital aspect of our life is also the most easily ignored: *breath*. In Genesis 2:7 ESV, "God formed the man of dust from the ground and breathed into his nostrils the breath of life, and the man became a living creature." We are made of mere dirt, alive solely by the breath of God. Our breath remains a sacred, constant generator of life—despite how little we consider it.

Our breath is the source of our energy. Biologically, it is where our life begins and ends. When we breathe deeply and slowly, our nervous system is shuttled into calmness. Contrarily, short, quick breaths drain our energy. Our tenseness is reflected in the tightness of our breath.

Breath is powerful, and its importance has been highlighted in a variety of activities and practices. Dancers, for example, are keenly aware of the connection between their breath and body. By lowering shoulders and breathing deeply while dancing, they can improve their balance and speed. Dancers with a heightened awareness of breath have greater stamina and performance.

Most meditative practices begin with calming our breath. When we become aware of our breath in meditation, we foster mental clarity, disconnect from tasks, and immerse ourselves within ourselves. In meditation, our breath is a simple yet unfailing anchor amid constant cognition.

Breath prayer is a Christian practice beginning in the sixth century, linking our breaths to our prayers to God. As we inhale, we may ask to receive a good thing of God: love, grace, or beauty. As we exhale, we release our disappointment, pain, and distraction to God. As we pray along the constant cadence of our breath, we position our spirits and bodies to fully receive God's peace.

The breath is not merely functional or siloed from our spiritual lives; it is a lasting, ever-present marker of God's nearness to us. As we become more aware of our breath, we become more aware of God, ourselves, and everything around us.

Awareness of Environment

Consider the vastness of a pale mountain adorned with golden clouds. The limber silhouette of a hawk slicing through a blank sky. The chorus of fresh rain crackling atop a ceiling. The scent of eucalyptus swelling across a street corner. Warm sunlight draped across our bodies like a blanket. Our surroundings can be an abounding source of gratitude, beauty, and peace—when we become aware of them. They form a holy bridge to God amid a distracted, hurried world.

Jesus upheld nature as a remedy to our anxieties. He says, "Look at the birds of the air: they neither sow nor reap nor gather into barns, and yet your heavenly Father feeds them... Consider the lilies of the field, how they grow: they neither toil nor spin, yet I tell you, even Solomon in all his glory was not arrayed like one of these" (Matt. 6:26, 28-29 ESV).

To Jesus, birdwatching is a spiritual discipline. Delighting in flowers is a spiritual discipline. Nature is not only worth noticing—it is abounding with wisdom for our lives. Our own stories are reflected in sprouting seedlings, blooming flowers, and towering oaks. Universal truths are written in the patterns of birds, the groupings of animals, and the life cycles of bacteria. But the environment we often occupy bears such little resemblance to the beautiful and good environment that God created.

The information age has forced much of our lives indoors and behind screens. It deceives us with unparalleled potential at our fingertips—yet empty, dissatisfied, mindless lives. We are more attuned to emails than flowers, notifications than birds, and to-do lists than sunsets. Even when we step outside, the temptation of our phones and stressors never leave us. But when we truly choose to become aware and consider the lilies, we regain our relationship to them. We cultivate awe. We discover God; we discover rest.

To become aware of our environment is to become aware of God. It requires stillness and mindfulness, not passive wandering. We might ask, what forms of life exist around us? What colors, textures, and forms of light do we observe? How is nature behaving around us? How might we consider the usual features of our environment more deeply—and see ourselves reflected in them?

Irish poet John O'Donohue often wrote of nature as being in conversation with us. He says in a 2008 interview, "When you wake in the morning and come out of your house, whether you believe you are walking into dead geographical location... or whether you are emerging out into a landscape that is just as much, if not more, alive as you, but in a totally different form, and if you go towards it with an open heart and a real, watchful reverence, that you will be absolutely amazed at what it will reveal to you... Landscape [isn't] just matter, but [it is] actually alive."[1]

When we feel burdened or restless, a simple stroll can recharge us far beyond our aimless scrolling on our phones. Transferring our attention to the all-too-familiar features of our environment brings us into the constant conversation of reality that we often ignore. Our environment is a sacred place, designed to be treated with care, wonder, and appreciation. In it, we will find rest.

Awareness of People

Just as we typically ignore our breath and environment, we similarly lack awareness of people. While listening to a friend, the buzzing of a phone captures our attention. When our children tell us stories, we murmur affirmations while mentally fixated on something else altogether. When engrossed in our own interests, we are prone to using others. Unfortunately, our own unawareness has significant consequences on others. But by practicing awareness of others, we can unwind our selfish fixations and experience relationships more fully.

Jesus practices this awareness of people throughout his life and ministry. In Mark 5, Jesus is described as being surrounded by a large crowd on his way to heal a synagogue leader's daughter. But when a desperate and bleeding woman crawls to touch the hem of his robe, he pauses. He immediately becomes aware of her, and even shifts his whole attention to her, calling her out from the crowd. Because of Jesus' awareness to this woman, she is healed.

Jesus exemplifies the quality of *interruptibility*, as he pauses from his task of healing to become present to the bleeding woman. We too, are called to be interruptible voyagers in a world occupied with self-interested pursuits. We are called to be aware of people and their needs, desires, and uniqueness. Even if, like Jesus, our goals are benevolent, we cannot ignore the person immediately beside us.

As we practice awareness of others, we also can enjoy the wonder of relationships—connection, healing, and compassion. The limits we often place on relationships are removed, and the joy and pain within them become more evident.

Awareness of Ourselves

Perhaps the most vital, yet most difficult, awareness we can cultivate is an awareness of *ourselves*.

Today, many people partake in varying pursuits of identity, affinity groups, and self-discovery. We fervently seek to find our "camp," and distinguish between who is inside and outside it. In doing so, our sense of ourselves becomes located not in self-awareness, but under the gaze and context of society.

Without awareness of self, we can even become strangers to our true selves. We fall victim to misunderstood motives and social signaling. We bend like dandelions in the wind, rather than being rooted like strong trees. Becoming aware of ourselves is a lifelong process requiring constant contemplation and revisiting. But Jesus offers guides and signposts along the journey.

In the 1981 film *Chariots of Fire*, runner Eric Liddell is reprimanded by his sister for focusing too much on running instead of his "responsibilities before God."[2] But Eric responds, "When I run, I feel His pleasure." Eric's awareness of himself enables him to pursue life-giving choices and connect with God. This simple awareness of pleasure and liveliness can help us discover where our soul thrives, and where we encounter God. The most life-giving moments we encounter are not always easy or carefree, but always meaningful. There, we experience a profound integration of our purpose, values, and existence. Similarly, we can ask and explore our inner places of pain, disappointment, and longing. This journey can be facilitated with practices like solitude, therapy, and reflective writing, and in it, we will find God.

The greatest gift we give ourselves in awareness is the knowledge that we are children of God, fully known and loved. When we rest in the awareness that we belong to God, we find the everlasting rest and peace that we are designed for.

03
Rest &
Resilience

Introduction

There is always so much that needs to be done. In our world, there is so much that is broken in need of mending, so many problems in need of solving, and so much pain crying out for a response.

Constantly responding to crisis takes a toll on our psyche. Our bodies release adrenaline, which triggers a pounding heart and shallow, rapid breathing. We become high-alert, acutely aware of potential threats. And while occasionally helpful, this state of being is not sustainable. After high-stress, fight-or-flight moments, we need to return to a *baseline*, where our nerves can "rest and digest." But most of us live in a state of chronic stress, avoiding the baseline. We waver between fatigue, slogging through mountains of tasks with ever-diminishing reserves of energy. We commonly experience burnout, being wholly depleted in mind, body, and spirit.

In this spent state, even the most heart-wrenching situations no longer evoke compassion—only numbness and dread. Our nerves are damaged; our bodies are ever on guard. Everything seems urgent—and resultantly, nothing seems urgent. We often feel incapable of responding or discerning how to offer the work of our hands.

The journey that Jesus calls us to is long. Late pastor Eugene Peterson called it "a long obedience in the same direction" and likened the journey to a pilgrimage, rather than a tourist jaunt.[1] The pilgrims in Psalm 84 are on the way to Zion, and they find resilience for the road by resting in God's strength. "As they go through the valley of Baca they make it a place of springs; the early rain also covers it with pools. They go from strength to strength; the God of gods will be seen in Zion" (Ps. 84:6-7 NSRV).

Yes, we are called to respond to the needs of this aching world. At the same time, God invites us to rest—to dip our souls into the springs of living water that he creates along the way. These two calls are not mutually exclusive, but sides of the same coin of discipleship. We must discover the rhythms of action and rest if we are to endure in the long, holy work of healing the world. We must discern what gives us strength and where we can find our own springs of spiritual, emotional, and physical refreshment.

Rest enables our resilience. In resting, we glimpse God as the author and center of rest, who calls us to his eternal rest. We are not there yet. We are pilgrims. But as we learn to rest on this journey, we will move from merely surviving to *thriving*.

Seasons of Rest

The Psalms opens with an image of trees "planted by streams of water, which yield their fruit in its season" (Ps. 1:3 NRSV). The trees do not produce year-round, but according to their growing cycle. This seminal book of worship, spanning the full range of human relationship with God, points us first to the wisdom of trees.

The trees observe the seasons: springs of new growth, summers of leafy abundance, autumns of loss and melancholy, and winters of inwardness and rest. The periods of barrenness and inactivity are as relevant and meaningful as those of outward extension and fruitfulness. Humans, who are also part of God's good creation, are designed for similar cycles. To be fruitful and whole, we must rest.

But our society has fallen stuck in one phase of the cycle: the *productive summer*. Busyness and having too little time is worn as a badge of honor, demarcating our importance. We feel guilty whenever we slow down. We itch to move on to the next thing. We reluctantly succumb to our bodies' needs for rest and sleep, or are forced to through illness or tragedy. Contrary to the cultural messages we receive, the *fall* and *winter* seasons are not optional. They are not inconvenient interruptions to our agenda, to what we "should" be doing. They are what we should be doing to live as God intended. In tree dormancy or human rest, little seems to be happening. But below the surface, deep transformation is underway.

Science is slowly registering what the psalmist already understood. Scientists have wondered for decades about the role of rapid eye movement, or REM sleep, which involves vivid dreaming and quick breathing. Some theorize that this phase helps consolidate memories, stimulates the central nervous system, and restores brain equilibrium. More recent research suggests that REM sleep activates many of the physical processes critical to healing from trauma.[2] In any case, it is clear that sleep is essential to our flourishing.

We also need time to rest while awake. When we're focused on a task, some parts of our brain go dark. These parts of the brain activate when we have unfocused downtime—that is, when we are alert but not doing something. It is the state where we daydream, reflect on the events of the day, and think about ourselves, our past, and our future. According to neuroscientists, this resting state of mind is crucial to developing empathy and a sense of self.[3]

In short, rest makes us more human. Rest nourishes us. Rest heals us. Rest changes us. Rest fosters new neural pathways, so that we make unexpected connections between things we did not realize were related. We see solutions to problems that seemed unsolvable.[4] Rest activates our imaginations away from the demands of our production-oriented society, and toward a fuller vision of God's abundant life—a life that involves seasons of fall and winter as much as seasons of spring and summer.

A Furnace of Transformation

As much as we may theoretically assent to our need for rest, we are emotionally unprepared to actually take our hand off the plough. In a society that values productivity above all else, our human worth has come to be defined by what we do. Who are we, if we are not our work, our incessant activity, or our accolades? When we do nothing, do we still matter?

Rest functions as what the Dutch priest Henri Nouwen called a "furnace of transformation." In the furnace, the false self built upon social expectations is exposed.[5] Without the whirring of computers, the clicking of emails shot off rapid-fire, and the ticking of to-do items running through our minds, we are left to face our own naked selves: angry, greedy, vulnerable, weak, desperate to hear others' praises, and yearning yet terrified to be fully known. It is no wonder we often avoid rest.

But in the quiet, as we reckon with what remains after our false selves have been exposed, God's word finally has a chance to break through. The prophet Isaiah declares, "All people are grass, their constancy is like the flower of the field. The grass withers, the flower fades, when the breath of the Lord blows upon it...but the word of our God will stand forever" (Is. 40:6-8 NRSV).

Rest, in its fullest sense, always leads us back to the steadfastness of God. Rest is not simply self-care, though it may involve aspects of that. The rest God calls us to involves dwelling "in the gentle healing presence of our Lord" and finding our "spiritual abode."[6] Nouwen writes, "As we come to realize that it is not we who live, but Christ who lives in us, that he is our true self, we can slowly let our compulsions melt away and begin to experience the freedom of the children of God."[7]

In God's rest, we are liberated to be who we truly are. We are *human*. We have limits. We are vulnerable. Though we try to be superhuman, we will always ultimately fail. And that is okay. We can do our work with gratitude and humility, knowing that it does not define our value. Only God's everlasting love defines us. Our fragile existence is held firmly in the center of God's hands.

As we rest in these truths, we are freed to respond to the needs of the world without the relentless demands of our society constraining our choices. We return to our work not out of compulsion and neediness, but out of the fullness of God that we have experienced.

Rest as Resistance

Rest is integral to the discipleship journey, enabling our resilience and freeing us from false selves to our true self in Christ. In another sense, rest is also an act of resistance to the powers that would exploit us.

Exploitation comes in many forms—some more subtle than others. When the Israelites were enslaved in Egypt, their exploitation was explicit, physical, and brutal. The Egyptian rulers, fearing the growing power of the descendants of Jacob, forced them into labor—building cities, making bricks, and working in the fields (Ex. 1:11-13). This work was clearly not for the Israelites' good, but to enrich the empire and oppress the Israelites.

Today, many of us toil as we believe we are expected to without asking whether it is for our good. What master are we serving? What ends are we working toward? Pharoah certainly did not have the Israelites' flourishing in mind, but today it is less clear whether our work is for our good. When we rest, we have a chance to probe these questions: *are we working toward flourishing, or are we being exploited?*

When Moses returned to Egypt after decades in exile, he asked Pharaoh to release the Israelites from their bondage to celebrate a festival to the Lord in the wilderness. "Why are you taking the people away from their work?" Pharaoh asked (Ex. 5:1-5 NRSV). Pharaoh's imperial machine had become too dependent on the Israelites' labor and could not afford their rest. In our analogous context, we often see ourselves as indispensable to the system. We do not question whether the system is designed for our good. We toil on, fearing that the show cannot go on without us. Though our work may feed our sense of self-worth—our false, egotistical self—if we cannot rest, we ultimately give in to exploitation.

In God's rest, we reclaim our true identity. We are formed not by the empire's expectations, but by worship and celebration. When we choose to rest, we may be called "lazy"—as the Egyptians called the Israelites—worthless, or making excuses not to work (Ex. 5:17 NRSV). But we must refuse to let our fear of what others say control us. We must refuse to let others' disapproval calibrate our worth.

No—we are not just cogs in the machine. We are no longer slaves. We are God's people. When the Israelites finally escaped Pharoah's grasp and entered the Promised Land, God instituted a weekly day of rest, the Sabbath, as a regular, embodied reminder. "Remember that you were a slave in the land of Egypt, and the LORD your God brought you out from there with a mighty hand and an outstretched arm; therefore, the LORD your God commanded you to keep the sabbath day" (Deut. 5:15 NRSV).

Today, we do not live in Pharoah's Egypt—but we still fall prey to oppressive forces that seek to define and control us. In rest, we claim an alternate identity. We do not belong to the systems of exploitation. We are free. We can rest. We can sleep. We can stop. We can honor the cycles of creation and our bodies. Each time we do so, we take one step closer along the pilgrimage to God's eternal rest.

04

Rest & Play

Introduction

In a culture that venerates profits and productivity, *play* requires a radical reordering of identity and life.

Even more than spiritual practices of solitude or silence, play is an immediate, holistic experience of *rest*. It is a natural process of releasing our tension and stimulating our senses. It accesses our imagination. It immerses our full selves—our bodies, our minds, our spirits—into experiences of delight.

Play invites us to shed the confines of productivity, performance, and prestige—and with these, our own egos and restlessness. It releases us from these common constrictions, reacquainting us with the wonder and joy we are designed to experience. In roaring laughter, unfiltered silliness, and whimsical activity, we experience the joys of merely *being*. We are suddenly freed from the world's constant demands. In play, our obsessions with image and output fade—and we are simply left with delight.

Play is an experience of our inner child, and it restores childlikeness in us. Of all people, children understand and exercise the profound wisdom of play. They have not yet unlearned nor reasoned themselves out of it. Their wisdom is innate; they act upon their instinctive hunger for play. Their giggles are unrestrained. They offer and receive invitations openly. They play until overcome with exhaustion—rising with continued hunger for play.

In the midst of his intense and important ministry, Jesus welcomed children. He paused to sit, speak, and play with them. While the society ignored and devalued children, Jesus prioritized them. His own disciples questioned this decision, as they anticipated no shortage of places to go and people to see. But however sensible, their logic was lacking. Jesus felt that children, along with their playfulness, were essential characters in his work.

"Jesus said, 'Let the little children come to me, and do not hinder them, for the kingdom of heaven belongs to such as these.' " – Matt. 19:14 NIV

Jesus welcomed the children, delighting in their company and playful presence. Might he have been modeling how it is to be rejuvenated by play? Perhaps, he was revealing that key aspects of his kingdom can only be accessed through the playful posture of a child. His choice demonstrates that play is worthwhile, even while engaged in the most important undertaking in history.

When we play, we are reminding ourselves of this. In a world dominated by seriousness and status, play is meaningful. It is where we release our burdens and actualize our identities as beloved children of God. It is where we experience God's lightness.

Rediscovering Play

Play is often absent from the norms and narratives of adult life. When practiced, it is understood as entertainment, consumption, or mere pleasure. But even in such things, few people feel rested, playful, and renewed by delight. Instead, we are misled to believe that we must spend lavishly, use substances, or impress others to experience "play."

Even in our normally "serious" spirituality, worship, and religion, we experience a great disassociation from play. The things of God are thought to be stoic and sober, so any pursuits of play take place *outside* of the context of spirituality. As we practice rest, we must examine these compulsions, structures, and narratives that ultimately hinder us from experiencing God in things like *play*.

"Therefore, since we are surrounded by such a great cloud of witnesses, let us throw off everything that hinders and the sin that so easily entangles. And let us run with perseverance the race marked out for us, fixing our eyes on Jesus, the pioneer and perfecter of faith." – Hebrews 12:1-2a NIV

The cultures of hurry, productivity, and performance easily entangle and burden us. Play is a quick method of throwing these off, enabling us to experience lightness of heart, mind, and body. In play, we find permission to lay down our burdens and return unencumbered to the God of grace, who renews our lives with true rest. Our attention does not wander to others' approval, but to Jesus. We can be unashamed.

When we embrace a robust theology of rest through play, we are moved beyond the falsehoods of productivity and "always having more to do." We begin and end in Jesus. Just as we delight, he delights in us.

While our work may yield beautiful, worthy offerings to the world—it is a fragile foundation for our meaning. Our souls yearn for us to lay down our tools and toil, and to experience the simple lightness and joys of play. Indeed, play is an antidote to burnout. When we play, we release what was never ours to hold. Our bodies exhale the tensions that bind us. We lay down our defenses and day planners, reborn into the living hope of Christ. In play, we refuse the urges to capitalize, monetize, or produce with our time, gifts, and hobbies. In play, we honor our inner child—the one who welcomes Jesus' sacred invitation to rest with him.

A Delightful World

In the 2020 Pixar film *Soul*, a soul named "22" enjoys her first taste of human life by accidentally occupying the body of pianist Joe Gardner.[1] As her initial sensations acquaint her to the reality of life, she is overtaken with awe. She curiously observes a maple leaf seed descending from a tree. She skeptically bites into a slice of greasy pizza, only to be thrilled by its flavors. She recognizes the "magic" of sitting and chatting in a barbershop chair, surrounded by listening ears. 22 is moved to pause and ponder the wonder of human existence because it is, indeed, *wonderful*.

Play involves recognizing the magic of life, and pausing to be awed or delighted in it. All humans are born with the capacity to delight. Even if the notion of extensive rest seems unrealistic, delighting only requires a moment of attention and a seed of joy. Do we recognize what enlivens our souls? Do we create space for such endeavors? We need not over-rationalize *why* we delight in God's handiwork; we must simply recognize that we are moved to delight, and embrace when we are.

Jesus, being in very nature God, delighted in time alone and with others. He frequented parties with eclectic batches of people, and insisted on good wine. He prepared feasts and prompted playful conversations with his beloved disciples. If God values delight in creation and people, how much more should we?

As 22 discovered on her first day on earth, life is *delightful*. Delight, while being a profoundly human experience, is often overlooked for distractions or digital dopamine-fixes. Play beckons us to recognize how our bodies delight in the taste of fresh fruit, the touch of a lover, or the thrill of a lively game of basketball. Play enables us to relish the daily delights of life. Play brings communities together in shared experiences of joy.

British writer C.S. Lewis famously wrote, "Joy is the serious business of heaven."[2] If our lives and labor do not prioritize joy, delight, and play, we will entirely miss the essential features of life with God.

A Grace of God

As a choice, play feels fickle next to more "important" pursuits or the many serious matters in the world. What business do we have in playing while others suffer or if important work is left undone? While play is no reason to ignore important action, its value cannot be discounted. Indeed, we live in a challenging world. And yet, we still find it within ourselves to laugh, delight, and play.

Swiss theologian Karl Barth writes, "Laughter is the closest thing to the grace of God."[3] Play can be a profound antidote to the callousness and coldness of an otherwise bleak world. Laughter itself is infectious, brightening an entire room of sullen faces. It is no wonder that a simple smile directed towards us—or worn on our own face—can drastically improve our mood. While tragedy and suffering are deeply human experiences, joy and play are as well.

In the field of trauma-informed therapy, practitioners have found play to be crucial in healing processes for children and even adults. Play is an unspoken language of the body, of the spirit. It involves a personal terrain untouched by words, which houses a hidden world of experience. By practicing play in the context of a trusted relationship, children can release and reset the trauma lodged in their minds. As they pull miniature cars across railings, give voice to plastic animals, and create new worlds with their imaginations, they experience healing.

When we excessively rationalize and spiritualize to make sense of our lives, we lose touch with this unspoken language. We must relearn *how to play*. We should consider resting in our "playgrounds," and allow our imaginations to flounder beyond their typical confines. We ought to let life's silly moments lead us into liturgies of unbridled laughter. We might even find that our work is most meaningful when we experience it, in some sense, as play.

Play can heal us. Play can give us rest. While we consider the many ways of resting with God, may we also allow ourselves to play and delight.

05

Rest & Community

Introduction

In the 1960s, mathematician and meteorologist Edward Lorenz theorized the *Butterfly Effect*—the concept that a tornado could be induced and influenced from the tiniest flap of the wings of a butterfly, weeks prior.

We live in an interconnected world. Our experiences and actions have tangible ramifications for those around us. Likewise, the activities of others have influence on us—our outlooks, perspectives, and ways of being. We are human beings that exist within a lattice of connections. We are humans that exist within *community*.

When we begin to consider rest within community, we find little reference in our world. Rest is most often articulated as something applied to the *individual*. Smartphone apps offer guidance for individual meditation, the "self-care" industry produces products to help individuals thrive, and even our practice of *The Sabbath* is most often understood as an *individualist* form of retreat with God.

This is ultimately not the full picture of the rest that God intends for us. The Bible is a text brimming with communities finding rest *together*. Abraham finds rest under a tree with three strangers (Gen. 18:1-8). Jesus reclines restfully over meals with his disciples (Matt. 26:17-30). Rest is a *collective experience;* we are invited to find rest amongst the kinship of others—and in turn, we are invited to help others rest.

Belonging

Rest within a community begins in the specific relationships of that community—the sacred bonds and threads that hold people together. Yet, relationships today often feel askew: we feel neglected, hurt, misunderstood, unworthy of love from others, or isolated from those around us. We become prone to perform, to please, and to perfect, mistakenly presuming that these things will lead us towards the loving relationships we long for. These exhausting activities lead us not only astray from the genuine relationships we seek, but towards perpetual agitation and strain—the opposites of rest.

Belonging is the essential value we crave. It is the primary experience of genuine rest within relationships. A mother cooking comfort food even after a long argument. A friend's loving, listening ear even after sharing something shameful. A community sharing support and resources towards someone in pain, even when receiving nothing in return. These moments exhibit *belonging*—relationships held together not by performative, transactional behaviors, but by mutual proclamation of sacredness, divinity, and preciousness in one another.

Jesus offers a rich narrative on belonging. In the *Parable of the Lost Son,* after shaming and squandering his father's wealth, the younger son decides to go back to his father in guilt and humiliation. He says, "Father, I have sinned against heaven and against you. I am no longer worthy to be called your son; make me like one of your hired servants" (Luke 15:18-19 NIV).

The younger son decides he is not worthy of belonging, and instead concludes that he must become a "hired servant". He believes that he must work and toil to experience even the slightest form of relationship with his father. Today, we are quick to do the same. In our relationships to others and God, we too feel we must prove our worth to others before we are able to experience *belonging.* We work and toil to feel connection. We rob relationships of their cosmic importance and reduce them to transactions. Any opportunity for rest becomes squandered in our endless, tireless efforts to feel loved.

But the father views the links between relationship, belonging, and rest alternatively to the son. When he sees the son in the distance, he runs towards him embracing and kissing him.

"'Quick! Bring the best robe and put it on him. Put a ring on his finger and sandals on his feet. Bring the fattened calf and kill it. Let's have a feast and celebrate. For this son of mine was dead and is alive again; he was lost and is found.' So they began to celebrate."
– Luke 15:22-24 NIV

The father's act expresses how rest manifests itself within relationships and communities of belonging: through wholehearted care. Feasts. Celebrations. Extravagance toward one another. Unconditional generosity. The younger son expects to labor and toil for connection—instead he is told to rest; he already belongs.

Rest arrives where belonging is present. Like the younger son, we are invited to be a part of relationships and communities that embrace belonging as something inherent and dignified for every human being. Rest is found here. Like the father, we are invited to foster these relationships and communities for others. We make spaces of rest for others when we express their belonging.

Delighting in Imago Dei

Rest is accessed in the present moment. In individualistic terms, this is straightforward: meditation teaches us to focus on breathing and minding the present moment, and our prayer times prompt us to be present with God. But what does it look like to practice presence amidst and with other human beings in community? We often perceive other people as *inhibitors,* instead of partners or prompters, in our ability to find rest. Our agendas and schedules clash, urgent attention is asked of us, and strong conflicts arise— all pulling us far from presence, and away from rest. How is *presence* found when we decide to involve other people?

In his famous commencement speech, "This Is Water," American writer David Foster Wallace describes to students a distraught depiction of adult life in which one finds themself in a "hideously, fluorescently lit" grocery store after a long day at work, full of irritating and annoying people.[1] We all too often find ourselves here, aggravated by those around us, finding them to be temporary friction points to be overcome on our way towards the perceived "deeper" and more "meaningful" experiences of presence and rest: quiet times, worship, journaling, sleep, etc.

Yet, Wallace challenges us that within the grocery store example, we have the choice to experience the situation and those around us differently:

"If I don't make a conscious decision about how to think and what to pay attention to… it's going to seem, for all the world, like everybody else is just in my way, and who are all these people in my way? But if you've really learned how to think, how to pay attention, then you will know you have other options. It will actually be within your power to experience a crowded, loud, slow… [grocery store] as not only meaningful but sacred, on fire with the same force that lit the stars—compassion, love, the sub-surface unity of all things."[2]

Being in relationship with God alters our understanding, perception, and attention towards others. People become divine, beautiful beings to be cherished as *Imago Dei*. The grocery store no longer becomes a place of relational friction. Instead, every tiny interaction and neighborly moment becomes an occasion to *delight* in another human being. Every sensation of annoyance towards another becomes an opportunity for compassion and empathy. These are the very things that generate *presence*.

Jesus always had people belaboring for his attention. Even when attempting to withdraw to a solitary place, crowds followed him. Yet, Jesus does not become irritated, frustrated, or impatient. Instead he sees everyone as *Imago Dei:*

"He withdrew by boat privately to a solitary place. Hearing of this, the crowds followed him on foot from the towns. When Jesus landed and saw a large crowd, he had compassion on them and healed their sick." – Matt. 14:13-14 NIV

Solitude and introversion are surely important practices to help us discover presence and rest for ourselves. But simultaneously, Jesus demonstrates that presence and rest can also be found in our posture towards others. Every relationship is an opportunity to delight in another—and as we do, we may find a deeper form of rest—one not tied to a specific restful practice, but in the abounding understanding that we are all connected to something larger than ourselves, brought together by the beauty and compassion of God.

Communities Oriented Around Rest

We understand most communities through the lens of their ambitions. Lofty church mission statements, formalized company values, and grand purposes all unify people in pursuit of a common goal. While these can be worthwhile pursuits, rest is typically viewed as *peripheral* in the narrative—secondary to whatever the larger determination or disposition is within the community.

While leading Israel through the wilderness, Moses reads a lofty statement of his own to all of Israel: "Observe the Sabbath day by keeping it holy, as the Lord your God has commanded you" (Deut. 5:12 NIV).

As Moses decrees this over the Israelite people, he is speaking to the priorities and organization of the community. Are our communities known by their productivity, efficiency, and charisma? Or are they known by how well they rest? Here, rest is not a pit stop towards advancing larger corporate goals—rest is at the heart of what defines a community.

"On [The Sabbath] you shall not do any work, neither you, nor your son or daughter, nor your male or female servant, nor your ox, your donkey or any of your animals, nor any foreigner residing in your towns, so that your male and female servants may rest, as you do. Remember that you were slaves in Egypt and that the Lord your God brought you out of there with a mighty hand and an outstretched arm. Therefore the Lord your God has commanded you to observe the Sabbath day."
– Deut. 5:15 NIV

Moses declares the very reason Israel must rest is because of their past experience of enslavement in Egypt. The Sabbath is a communitywide declaration that they are now *free*. This rest is not reserved for a few—but for children, servants, foreigners, and even animals. Here, Moses prophetically calls the entire society to be oriented around rest, because rest reminds them of their corporate identity as a free people.

Likewise, we are invited to sponsor this form of rest within our own relationships and communities, and to declare this freedom tangibly for others. We do this by creating spaces, structures, and cultures that allow others to rest, providing resources and reparations for those who do not have the means to rest well, and feasting together as a celebratory form of rest. In all our relationships, we demonstrate to people their worth and belonging, so that they may rest wholeheartedly.

We are interconnected beings. Our postures, our actions, our own abilities to rest all touch, inform, and influence the living communities around us. As we bring about rest in the relationships around us, we alter the narrative of what truly matters in the world.

06
Rest & Pace

Introduction

Hurry is a way of life.

We live in a world that glamorizes overworking, efficiency, and expediting results. Society moves at a pace faster than our humanity and health can sustain. Like a frog in slowly-boiling water, we are largely unaware of our environs gradually strangling us as we toil to maintain the engines of industry. Our frantic busyness threatens to define us, as we are tempted to believe the old adage—"we are what we repeatedly do"—and we simply do too much.

While we have normalized low-grade anxiety and a constant state of stress, Jesus embodies a different way of living. When asked what single word he would use to describe Jesus' time on earth, philosopher Dallas Willard famously responded: "relaxed."[1] Jesus' life was world-changing and salvific—but it was also *slow*.

When we observe the unhurried pace at which Jesus lived, walked, and worked, we encounter the slow-moving God— one that longs for true, fulfilling rest for our starved souls. In Jesus, rest becomes more than temporary respite, but a road to freedom from an ailing society burdened by speed and productivity. Rest becomes an invitation to decelerate and partake in the simple but hallowed act of *being*.

The Slow-Moving God

"And the Spirit immediately drove him out into the wilderness. He was in the wilderness forty days, tempted by Satan; and he was with the wild beasts; and the angels waited on him."
– Mark 1:12-13 NRSV

Many regard Jesus' stint in solitude as the inaugural act of his three-year ministry. We can imagine this must have bemused Jewish contemporaries—or even modern-day scholars—as the wilderness does not appear a premier location for the Messiah's first mission. Surely, Jerusalem would be the more sensible choice—there is ample work to be done there! What work did he do in the wilderness?

Throughout his life, Jesus confounded his companions and students at every stop and turn. On one account, Jesus was en route to visit the daughter of Jairus, an important religious, political figure of the time. Even as she lay deathly ill and in need of emergency assistance, Jesus stopped in his tracks. He paused his urgent assign-

ment for a woman on the streets—an outcast ostracized and despised because of her sickness—and listened to her life story. No matter the circumstance, Jesus took his time.

In another case, when learning his friend Lazarus was on the brink of death, Jesus waited another *two days* before traveling to see him. The Savior took inconvenient detours in his ministry, often retreating to desolate places to pray. Even when a storm threatened to sink his disciples' boat, Jesus was soundly asleep. Even when situations were the most dire, Jesus was never rushed.

Having journeyed with Jesus for years, his disciples must have been fraught with frustration and impatience. Even now, observing Jesus' behavior exasperates and confuses us. Had we conducted quarterly reports on Jesus' productivity, we may have been skeptical of his impact and efficiency. We would have certainly questioned why he did not do more.

Why would Jesus spend forty days by himself? Isn't a weekend enough? Why did he wait 30 years to begin his ministry? Couldn't he have started at 18? Why does God wait to save the world?

When Jesus stops on the road to spend supper in someone's home, we dismiss those moments as "interruptions" to his ministry at large. In a culture that confuses slowness with laziness and dimness, we gloss over Jesus' silent miracles and fixate on other, more grandiose moments. But Jesus' slowness is intentional and prophetic, quietly subverting our value systems, our notions of importance, and our ideas of who a Savior should be. It reveals how we have warped time and distorted our priorities. Jesus' relaxed pace is a direct challenge to our cultural pace, which measures our worth by achievements and not our inherent dignity.

When we walk with a slow God, we realize that *being*—not *doing*—with people was Jesus' ministry. Only when we perceive this can we be nourished by the hospitality of someone who society convinced us was an enemy. Only when we sit still can we be humbled and changed to see those deemed invisible by society. Only when we follow this pace can we experience Jesus' solidarity in our own mourning, and his redemptive power in desperate circumstances.

A hurried heart cannot see the slow-moving God and a hurried heart cannot rest.

If *being* was Jesus' ministry, it did not begin in the wilderness, but when he became incarnate thirty years earlier. Jesus was preemptively named *Immanuel* because Immanuel means "God with us." Jesus did not lose his divinity when he slowed down—rather, he became fully human. His incarnation demonstrates to us that rest is about presence. It is about returning to our whole selves. Living at Jesus' restful pace is about becoming fully human again.

We may romanticize ideas of "running after God" and "doing the Lord's work." But love is not rushed. If we are misguided by efficiency, external results, and doing more for God, we will leave love behind. God is in no hurry to save the world. And if we choose to partner with him, we partake in something larger than ourselves—a movement that spans millennia, governed by the pace of love.

Practicing Presence

Being with God means walking at his pace, but our steps are misaligned and frantic. Reeling from the whiplash of a hurried society, we forget our divine longing for presence and cannot stand the intolerable weightlessness of sitting still.

We are handcuffed by our watches. We publicly boast of our overbooked agendas while internally loathing our chronic anxiety and unhappiness. *Time* and the way we spend it becomes a rigid moral evaluation of our character for others to critique. Busyness makes us feel needed and important. It tempts us with hollow promises of worth and prestige, as if doing more signifies *being more*. We believe the story: if I am not saturating my schedule to its limits, then I am not doing all that I can to be a good worker, a good partner, a good friend, a good parent—really, anything good. If I do not do enough, I am not *enough*.

The sad irony of our condition is that this frenzied pace does not make us more whole—but the opposite. Despite its shiny facade, busyness fails us. Stretching ourselves beyond our limits and working more does not equip us better to love, to freely hand out grace, to forgive, or to offer compassion. Instead, it leads us to unhealthy cycles of anxiety, stress, and self-concern. Contrary to our expectations, it renders our souls brittle and malnourished.

To experience an alternate, liberated pace in life—free from norms of hurry and strain—we not only need a God who is unbound by our temptations of hurry, but a God who *loves*. A God who can do everything and can be anywhere at all times, yet chooses a pace of life that accepts being present in only *one* body. Through Jesus' life, we can observe how God might live had he been in our condition—breathing, eating, sweating, working, commuting, walking, sleeping. What might an all-powerful God do if he had "too much to do and too little time"?

When we look closely at Jesus' lifestyle, we will notice that his priorities were not like our own, but divorced from economic incentives, political pressures, and the expectations of his peers. Jesus set his own rhythm, independent of his surroundings, stopping and proceeding at his own judge-ment. His uncanny pace and "work-life balance" should challenge us. It should beg the question: if Jesus walked leisurely in his work, why am I *running?*

Perhaps we have not only said yes to too many things, but we have said yes to the wrong things. Jesus noticed people, and he slowed down—stopping, often—for them. Jesus exposed to us the inflated im-portance of our agendas and demonstrat-ed how to be interruptible. He valued work, but emphasized that we are never too busy to extend kindness and help to someone in need. Contrary to our socie-tal deception, work can wait.

Like Jesus, we too have direct access to the same God of presence—the one who guided his steps and set his tempo. We too have the agency to practice an alternate pace, synced to the rhythm of God. For some, this may require establishing firm work boundaries or setting limits on com-mitments. Whatever it is, we ought to prac-tice a pace that facilitates presence: to our spirits, our health, and our communities.

In Spirit

Practicing breathing exercises, journaling, or meditating before our daily bustle are all ways to be present to our inner-selves. When we create spaces of stillness and quiet, we are attuned with our beings—the essence of ourselves. This awareness equips us to bet-ter tend to our soul's needs, listen to its cries, and hear what God is saying of them.

In Body

Too often, Christians over-spiritualize our lives and character formation, forgetting that God entrusted us with bodies. We toil and push towards "good causes," ignorant of how accelerated our heart rates have be-come or how short our breaths are. But we will not be whole unless our bodies, too, are whole. Creating a consistent sleeping sched-ule, not skipping meals, taking daily walks, and exercising are all rhythms we can imple-ment in our daily lives to care for and nour-ish our physical beings.

In Community

Allowing Jesus to minister to us in our inner and physical lives upholds our availability to our families, loved ones, and communities. We can depart from a deficit-mindset—being stingy with our time, energy, and generosity—and towards a posture of abundance. We can practice presence in our communities by finding creative ways to serve and be attentive to them, whether advocating for neighbors in need, practicing active listening with friends, or remaining interruptible to daily needs around us.

In Work

In practicing a pace of presence in our spirits, our bodies, and our communities, we can then be present to our work. In an order much like this, our priorities can be realigned and we notice what Jesus noticed; we are led to stop and go on his cue. We receive perspective of our place as children of God in a movement beyond ourselves. This affirmation of identity and worth sets the precedence for our work—

not the other way around. Only then are we truly free from the yoke of labor; only then are we our whole selves.

True rest cannot be compartmentalized into a neat schedule, because presence is holistic. The Sabbath will not only set a unique pace for our off-days; it is meant to permeate our entire lifestyle. As we practice presence, we are mobilized into a new rhythm fit to partner with God: a walking pace.

Wasting Time

"But when Jesus saw this, he was indignant and said to them, 'Let the little children come to me; do not stop them; for it is to such as these that the kingdom of God belongs. Truly I tell you, whoever does not receive the kingdom of God as a little child will never enter it.'" – Mark 10:14-15 NRSV

For brevity's sake, only Jesus' most noteworthy moments are recorded in the gospel accords—the baptism of Jesus, Jesus performing miracles, Jesus clashing with the religious elite, and the like. But how often do we ponder the more ordinary times of his life, the "moments in between moments?" What was it like when Jesus was walking from city to city with his followers? How did they hold small talk on those long treks?

Rarely do we consider that following Jesus can mean living at an ordinary, mundane, or even *wasteful* pace with him. Even in our rest, we expect a theatrical, mountain-top experience to change our lives in dramatic fashion. But rest is not about changing our lives—at least not in the grandiose way we expect.

We are often unable to see the merit of doing "nothing" with God, or with ourselves. We cannot indulge in the simple joy of watching grass grow or sitting still for hours before our souls get fidgety with the impending dread to optimize our lives. A pastime cannot simply be *that*, before it is pivoted and capitalized into a side hustle.

How often do we grant ourselves the permission to be bad at something? To relish in singing off-key or messing up a new recipe? How have we deprived ourselves of the enjoyment of unoptimized time—time that doesn't serve to make us better assets in the workforce, better friends, better bosses, or better parents? Journalist Rainesford Stauffer, an advocate for wasting time, puts it aptly: "The glory of the silly hobby lies in not proving anything, not even that you can do it, because it doesn't matter if you can."[2]

Living work-oriented lives, we have co-opted rest into a means to simply work more. It has become nothing more than a respite to re-charge and re-energize. We rush into rest and attempt to expedite its results, as if trying to fall asleep by sheer will. We use prayers as incantations to manufacture rest and fabricate spiritual outcomes. Self-care is conspicuous, measurable, and shareable—otherwise, it is a "waste of our time."

But rest happens not when we've done enough "restful things" or when God gives us a life-changing revelation, but when we've learned to release. Rest happens when we suspend all our weight into freefall.

Rest needs no justification other than *itself*. It is not a means to an end; it is the means *and* the end. Rest does not exist for work, but it exists because it is inherently good. No amount of work we accomplish will earn us rest, because rest is our universal birthright.

Perhaps this is what Jesus meant when he said children have special access to his kingdom. Perhaps this is why Jesus' message felt so threatening and unacceptable: it renders all of our culturally-assigned symbols of worth obsolete. It thwarts our value systems and arbitrary standards of importance; it makes us bare.

Children are humanity in its most frank and undisguised condition—they mirror our truest and most vulnerable parts of ourselves. A child plays, not because they've earned it, but simply because of who they are. In our most stripped selves, we don't work for God—we play with God. We go on long walks with him, gaze at beautiful scenery together, and exchange our imaginations with him.

Botching an art project or messing up a dance choreography feels meaningful because it is not supposed to be. There is hidden grace in reveling in wasted time and in making mistakes without much consequence, as if signaling to us that there is worth in who we are—as our incomplete, unfinished selves. We are free to commit the hallowed act of *being;* we are ushered into wholeness.

Slowing down is a spiritual practice. It is a necessary healing balm for a people nauseated from the rush of a world that strips them of their humanity. The pace of leisure is a pace of resistance. When we slow down, we tap into our forgotten, but innately-human longing for presence, placed within us by the slow-moving God. When we live at the pace of love, we find that God is also longing for presence. He is pining for us, yearning to be with us again.

07

Rest & Changing the World

Introduction

Rest is a satisfying balm. It is a place of refuge for aching bodies, weary souls, and foggy minds. It renews, restores, and rebuilds. It is an essential practice for how *all* of creation thrives—not only humanity.

Consider the *soil*. While most societies have departed from agrarian lifestyles, farmers and caretakers of the earth understand the need for the soil to rest. Farming practices like *fallowing* allow soil to rest, free of sowing and reaping. In rest, soil is cleansed of toxic pathogens, recovers its organic matter, and replenishes its biodiversity. The ceremonial laws of ancient Israel prescribed similar practices for treatment of the land.

"For six years you are to sow your fields and harvest the crops, but during the seventh year let the land lie unplowed and unused. Then the poor among your people may get food from it, and the wild animals may eat what is left. Do the same with your vineyard and your olive grove." – Ex. 23:10-11 NIV

In a model evocative of the seventh-day Sabbath, God instructs Israel to allow the ground to rest on the seventh year. People and animals were to enjoy its fruits. For an entire year, "perfectly good" soil would be undisturbed and unused. For Israel's agrarian society, this seven-year cycle enforced significant limits on the economy and pace of the nation. Without any such rest, the society could maintain high standards of production and consumption. But the soil would decay, unable to properly absorb water or yield crops.

By resting the land, the marginalized of Israel's society would benefit and the land would be restored to its natural balance and enriched. While botanically wise, this practice was included as a way of honoring God. Soil, dirt, crops, and seeds—these things of the earth were not separate from the things of God, but a key feature of worship.

As creatures crafted of soil, we are not unlike the land in our need for rest. But instead of personal and societal practices reflective of the Sabbath, we endlessly till and plow. We do not allow the land to rest, nor do we allow ourselves to rest. In return, the world's wildlife, forests, oceans, and skies groan in exhaustion, and human hearts echo this groan. We aspire to innovate ourselves beyond these behaviors, but reliably fall prey to them. We repeat the sins of our ancestors, endlessly trapped by the consequences of our own selfishness, exploitation, and weariness. *We* need to rest.

Rest is a Blessed Thing

In Genesis, we find the world's beginning as formless and empty. God begins to create and fill the structures, beings, and processes of creation. On the seventh day of the creation story, God rests.

"Then God blessed the seventh day and made it holy, because on it he rested from all the work of creating that he had done." – Gen. 2:2 NIV

God's final act of creation was to bless and declare the seventh day as *holy* because of rest. God, with infinite and endless power and ability to create all things from nothing, saw it fit to take a break.

The holiness of God's rest escapes our theologies and societal norms. We honor the contributions of our premier leaders, thinkers, entrepreneurs, artists, and athletes for their ingenuity, work ethic, and accomplishments—not their decisions to *rest*. While applauding the contributions of people and societies is no bad thing, our valuations of work and rest are lopsided. By valuing production above all else, we perpetuate cycles of exploitation and exhaustion. We ignore these consequences, and instead think of rest as wasteful, inefficient, and costly.

In the creation story, God demonstrates an obvious value and passion for work. God spends six days busily creating—but God is not bound by work nor worships it. While declaring all of creation to be good, God reserves a special blessing of holiness for the seventh day of rest. Rest is a blessed thing. It is declared holy by God.

The creation story has profound implications for our spiritual and physical lives. Rest is not a luxury, afterthought, or feature of entertainment. It is an essential, holy aspect of life as it was meant to be. Rest is a blessed dimension of reality. Everyone and everything, everywhere, is designed to rest: land, creatures, and people alike.

When we live into this precedent, we more closely embody the world as God intends. We are less irritable parents. We are more hospitable homes. We are kinder stewards of the earth. We are more just societies. We are more *human*. It is when we choose to orient our lives, communities, and institutions around rest, that we may finally glimpse the quieting of a groaning world.

Rest is Resistance

For better or worse, our societies work to survive. The typical person dreams of the day their dues of working are paid, when they might finally rest and enjoy the fruits of their labor. This notion of retirement evokes images of leisure, entertainment, and recreation with loved ones. Yet the promise of such a season is waning.

In the United States, only a quarter of all employees are guaranteed lifelong retirement benefits—and employers are increasingly opting out of this.[1] Along with limited state benefits, rising medical costs, and economic downturns, older generations struggle to secure a safe future for themselves and younger generations remain trapped in despair. Retirement, an institutional symbol of rest, is becoming more vulnerable by the year.

This is but one symptom of a profound misalignment of societal values. Our idolatry of production has created record inequality, widespread poverty, and declining prospects of a bright future. While work was designed to dignify humanity and enable communities to thrive, we have twisted and abused it into a deeply harmful thing. There is no shortage of oppression, exploitation, and dehumanization in our corporatist and consumerist world. This complex perpetuates norms of hurry, anxiety, and fear, which dominate our lives from beginning to end.

Modern industrialized nations are not alone in their habits of exploitation and greed. The book of Exodus details how the pharaohs of Ancient Egypt enslaved and exploited Israelites as objects of back-breaking production. In his book *Sabbath as Resistance,* theologian Walter Brueggeman confronts

Pharaoh's worldview of insatiable production with God's worldview of "neighborliness." He writes, "The Sabbath rest of God is the acknowledgement that God and God's people in the world are not commodities to be dispatched for endless production and so dispatched, as we used to say, as 'hands' in the service of a command economy. Rather they are subjects situated in an economy of neighborliness."[2]

While an economy of anxiousness whips all people into a pursuit of "more" by any means necessary, an economy of neighborliness *elevates* the people engaged in the work—not the work itself, nor the products of their labor. This is emphasized in Exodus 23:10-12, where God commands the land to rest so that the community around it—the poor, foreigners, and animals—shall be refreshed by it. This communal disposition is fiercely opposed to any empire's obsession with production. Thus, the Sabbath is the ultimate form of resistance. It resists the norms of anxiety, endless ambition, and constant demands. It resists the economic forces of greed, exploitation, and degradation of people and land. It resists the gods of power and money. It is a day of sacred remembrance that we belong to God and each other—and are not merely meant for production.

"Remember that you were slaves in Egypt and that the LORD your God brought you out of there with a mighty hand and an outstretched arm. Therefore the LORD your God has commanded you to observe the Sabbath day." – Deut. 5:15 NIV

After 400 years of cruel enslavement, Israelites primarily understood themselves as slaves. The Sabbath was a liberatory reminder that they were free of that identity; that they were God's people. By observing rest, the Israelites continuously redefined themselves against the lingering wounds of enslavement.

Today, the Sabbath rest is still a matter of our identity. Are we objects of production or beloved image-bearers of God? Will our society be known and evaluated for its monetary successes or its compassion for the most vulnerable? In exchange for an anxiety-ridden life predicated on the flimsy foundations of financial gain, we are invited into a Sabbath rest that enjoys thriving relationships with God and neighbor. When we embody this rest, we remember who we are and what we are made for amidst a world that constantly tells us otherwise.

A Beautiful Future

The Hebrew word for rest is *shabbat,* which we under-stand as ceasing from work. But another Hebrew word for rest is *nuakh,* which can mean to dwell or settle in. This word appears after the creation of man.

"The Lord God took the man and put (nuakh) him in the Garden of Eden to work it and take care of it." – Gen. 2:15 NIV

The man is made to *dwell* in the garden, where he works and cares for the creation. The *nuakh* rest is not occa-sional or marginal, but a complete posture of life. It is not a weekend endeavor, but a central force and energy that directs the life and purpose of all things.[2] It is not a "pit stop" on the road to doing, but it is a place of dwelling and settling. And it is this kind of rest that changes the world.

Rest is God bending the universe towards love, peace, justice, and Shalom. *Rest* is the return to a divine time, energy, and reality. *Rest* is the ushering forth of a beau-tiful reality predicated on more than the work of our hands. *Rest* is a blessed thing.

When we participate in rest—all its holiness, aware-ness, resilience, play, community, pace, and resistance—we create a more beautiful world together. We heal our wounds. We rest our anxious hearts. We liberate ourselves from the forces of exploitation. We discover the slow, delightful, transformative life we were designed to live. And we rest *with God*.

May God move us towards rest. *Amen.*

 ALABASTER

**PRODUCT & PHOTOGRAPHY
SPECIALIST**
Samuel Han

**EDITOR-IN-CHIEF
& HEAD OF WRITING**
Daniel Sunkari

**CO-FOUNDER
& CREATIVE DIRECTOR**
Bryan Ye-Chung

PRODUCT MANAGER
Tyler Zak

**LAYOUT & COVER
DESIGN**
Grace Susilo

COVER IMAGE
Anna Letson

**CO-FOUNDER
& MANAGING DIRECTOR**
Brian Chung

FINANCE & TALENT DIRECTOR
Willa Jin

**OPERATIONS & CUSTOMER
EXPERIENCE DIRECTOR**
Emaly Hunter

MARKETING ASSOCIATE
Emma Tweitmann

CONTENT ASSISTANT
Darin McKenna

WRITERS

Adaobi Ugoagu (Ch. 7)

Alana Freitas (Ch. 1)

Bryan Ye-Chung (Ch. 5)

Daniel Sunkari (all)

Kayla Craig (Ch. 4)

Lillian Chen (Ch. 2)

Liuan Huska (Ch. 3)

Justin Lee (Ch. 6)

PHOTOGRAPHERS

Ally Wei

Anna Letson

Brandon Cook

Brenda Palencia

CJ Lanon

Darien Henson

Echo Chen

Heidi Parra

Joel Schat

Jonathan Knepper

Joshua Martens

Mac Elliott

Makito Umekita

Mike Sunu

Naomi Zaki

Samuel Han

ENDNOTES

1 | REST & GOD

1. Calhoun, Adele Ahlberg. *Spiritual Disciplines Handbook: Practices That Transform Us.* InterVarsity Press, 2015.
2. Odell, Jenny. *How to Do Nothing: Resisting the Attention Economy.* Melville House, 2019
3. *Ibid.*
4. Calhoun, *Spiritual Disciplines Handbook.*

2 | REST & AWARENESS

1. Tippett, Krista and John O'Donohue. "The Inner Landscape of Beauty." *On Being with Krista Tippett.* 28 Feb. 2008. Accessed 2021. https://onbeing.org/programs/john-odonohue-the-inner-landscape-of-beauty-aug2017/.
2. Hudson, Hugh, director. *Chariots of Fire.* 20th Century Fox, 1981.

3 | REST & RESILIENCE

1. Peterson, Eugene H. *A Long Obedience in the Same Direction: Discipleship in an Instant Society.* 40th Anniversary Commemorative Ed. (Downer's Grove, IL: InterVaristy, 2019), 9-12.
2. Vitelli, Romeo. "Exploring the Mystery of REM Sleep." *Psychology Today.* 25 March 2013. Accessed 11 May 2021. https://www.psychologytoday.com/us/blog/media-spotlight/201303/exploring-the-mystery-rem-sleep.
3. Stixrud, William and Ned Johnson. *The Self-Driven Child: The Science and Sense of Giving Your Kids More Control Over Their Lives.* (New York: Viking, 2018), 136-138. See also: Raichle, Marcus E. "The Brain's Dark Energy." *Scientific American.* March 20120, 44-49.
4. Levitin, Daniel. *The Organized Mind: Thinking Straight in the Age of Information Overload.* New York: Dutton, 2014.
5. Nouwen, Henri. *The Way of the Heart: Connecting With God Through Prayer, Wisdom, and Silence.* (New York: Ballantine Books, 1981), 15-22.
6. Nouwen, 21.
7. Nouwen, 20.

4 | REST & PLAY
1. *Soul.* Directed by Pete Docter and Kemp Powers, Walt Disney Pictures and Pixar Animation Studios, 2020.
2. Lewis, C. S. *Letters to Malcolm: Chiefly on Prayer.* William Collins, 2020.
3. Barth, Karl. Unknown.

5 | REST & COMMUNITY
1. Wallace, David Foster. "This is Water". Little, Brown, 2009.
2. *Ibid.*

6 | REST & PACE
1. Willard, Dallas. Unknown.
2. Stauffer, Rainesford. "The Joy of Being Bad at Something." *Human Parts.* 20 Jan. 2020. Accessed 2021. https://humanparts.medium.com/the-joy-of-being-bad-at-something-ee8b4cec9952.

Sources:
    An Unhurried Life, Alan Fadling
    Mark 1:12-13 (NIV)
    Mark 10:14-15 (NIV)

7 | REST & CHANGING THE WORLD
1. "What Statistics Does the BLS Provide on Frozen Defined Benefit Plans?" *U.S. Bureau of Labor Statistics.* www.bls.gov/ncs/ebs/factsheet/defined-benefit-frozen-plans.htm.
2. "Two Kinds of Work - 7th Day Rest E3." *Bible Project Podcast.* The Bible Project. 28 October 2019. Accessed 2021. https://thebibleproject.simplecast.com/episodes/two-kinds-of-work-7th-day-rest-e3-ugWTiK84.

WWW.ALABASTERCO.COM